Vocal physiology and the teaching of singing : a complete guide to teachers, students, and candidates for the A.R.C.M., L.R.A.M., and all similar examinations

David D Slater

VOCAL PHYSIOLOGY

VOCAL PHYSIOLOGY

AND THE

TEACHING of SINGING.

A Complete Guide to Teachers, Students

AND

CANDIDATES

For the A.R.C.M., L.R.A.M.,

AND

ALL SIMILAR EXAMINATIONS.

BY

DAVID D. SLATER, A.R.C.M.

ONE SHILLING & SIXPENCE, NET.

LONDON:

J. H. LARWAY,

14, WELLS STREET, OXFORD STREET, W.

Lowe & Brydone Printers Ltd.,
Typographical Music and General Printers,
Victoria Road, Willesden Junction, N.W.10.

PREFACE.

WHILE the primary object of this little book is to assist and guide Students in preparing for the A.R.C.M., L.R.A.M., **and all similar examinations,** it is hoped that it may also prove useful to Teachers and Students of singing generally.

The book is divided into three parts:—

PART I. is a short, but comprehensive treatise on **Vocal Physiology.**

> There are already many excellent books on this subject, some of which may be read by Students with great profit, but in these pages the Author has endeavoured to set forth the main facts, avoiding unnecessary matter, yet *covering all the ground required for examination and practical purposes.*

PART II. is designed to assist the Candidate in the **Paper Work** of his examination.

> It must be remembered, however, that the paper work in the examinations of the various colleges varies more or less, and the Candidate must study the syllabus of the particular examination for which he is entering, so that he may know, precisely, what is required of him.

PART III. is devoted to the **Oral Examination.**

> In it the Candidate is instructed in the method of procedure adopted in the examination room. Thereafter, all the most important points connected with voice production are thoroughly dealt with, including the commonest faults, and the remedies for them.

On comparing the syllabus of the Royal College (A.R.C.M.) with that of the Royal Academy, (L.R.A.M.) it will be found in the latter, that Candidates must sing a *Recitative,* a portion of a *Cantabile Movement,* and a portion of a *Florid Movement*, selected by them-selves from the lists given, while in the former this is not required. Apart from this, the oral examinations for these diplomas are very similar.

The main subjects on which questions will be asked are stated in the syllabi, but it must be clearly understood that there are many questions attached to each subject, and that the very answering of these, will, or may, give rise to side questions. These side questions will depend largely on the answers given by the Candidate to the leading questions, hence the necessity for a comprehensive and thorough knowledge of the whole subject.

Many of the points which have been dealt with in Part III. may never be touched upon, but there is not one of them but should be known and thoroughly understood by every teacher of singing. Then, again, any of these questions might be given for treatment in the paper-work examination.

Candidates are strongly advised to obtain the assist-ance of a good *Coach*. Many excellent teachers of singing make a speciality of this work, and will instruct candidates, either personally or by correspondence.

The Author begs to acknowledge his indebtedness to Mr. S. W. Churchill, L.R.A.M., A.R.C.M., a specialist on these Examinations, for much valuable information.

The following books will be found useful in study :—

"First Principles of Music."—Manhire. *(Larway).*
"Musical Ornaments."—Harding. *(Weekes).*
"Harmony" (Primer No. 8).—Stainer. *(Novello).*
"Speech in Song" (Primer No. 6).—Ellis. *(Novello).*
"Voice, Song and Speech" (For Vocal Physiology).— Brown & Behnke. *(Sampson, Low, Marston & Co.).*
"Hints on Singing."—Manuel Garcia. *(Ascherberg, Hopwood & Crew).*
"Singing" (Primer No. 5).—Randegger. *(Novello).*
"The Singer's Guide."—Adcock. *(Curwen).*
"Grammar of Elocution."—Millard. *(Longmans, Green & Co.).*

DAVID D. SLATER

CONTENTS.

LIST OF PLATES.

PART I.

VOCAL PHYSIOLOGY.

THE CHEST OR THORAX.

The trunk of the body is divided into two main compartments; viz., the Chest above, and the Abdomen below.

These two compartments are separated from each other by a *strong muscular* partition called the Diaphragm.　(Fig. I., D.).

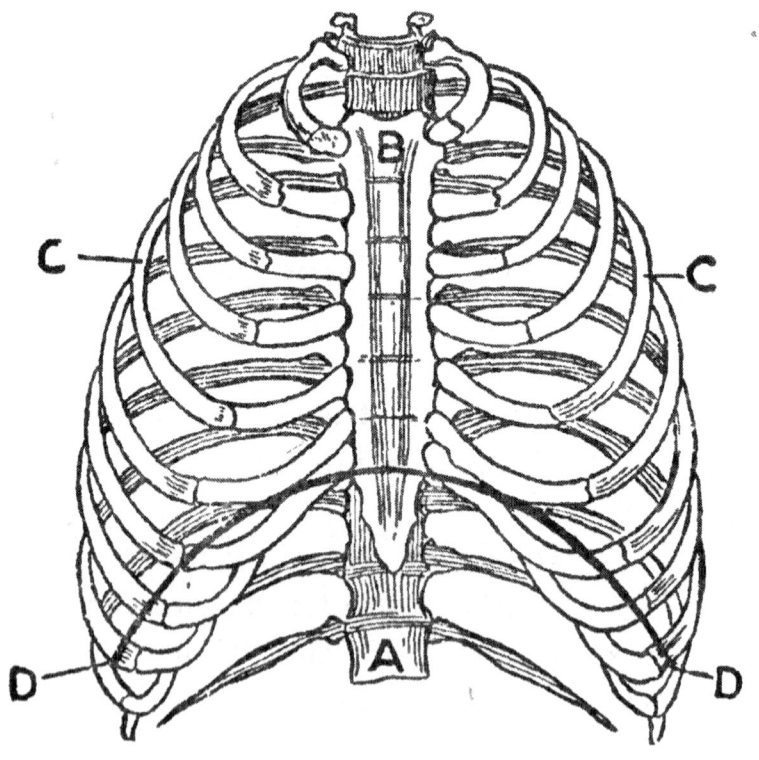

Fig. I.　The Framework of the Chest.
A, Spine.　B, Breastbone.　C, Ribs.　D, Diaphragm.

The **Diaphragm** forms the floor of the chest and the roof of the abdomen, and in repose is *dome-shaped*, presenting a *convex surface to the chest*, and a *concave one to the abdomen*.

When contracted, it *flattens*, and *presses down upon the abdominal organs*. (See page 30).

The framework of the Chest (Fig. I.) is formed by—

The Spine, (behind)

. The Breastbone or Sternum, (in front) and

The Ribs, (twelve on either side).

This framework presents the appearance of a cone-shaped cage, formed by two uprights—. one behind, *(The Spine)* one in front, *(The Breastbone)*, and a series of hoops or rings *(The Ribs)* of different diameters, the smallest being at the top and the largest at the bottom.

From this description it will be easily understood that the *internal capacity of the Chest* is *greatest below*, and *least above*.

All the ribs are attached to the spine by movable joints, which permit of their being raised or lowered at will.

The seven upper ribs, on each side, are attached to the breastbone *by cartilage*.

The eighth, ninth and tenth are attached in front to each other by a *cartilaginous band*.

The eleventh and twelfth are much shorter, and do not reach round to the front. They are free, or unattached, at their forward ends, and so are called the *floating ribs*.

The ribs do not stand out at right angles from the spine and breatbone, but *droop downwards at the sides*.

They are supplied with an inner and an outer set of muscles, which are called the *intercostal muscles*.

The *outer intercostals* raise the ribs.

The *inner intercostals* pull down the ribs.

This subject will be dealt with under "Breathing." (See page 30).

THE LUNGS.

The Lungs (Fig., II. A, B.) are two cone-shaped objects, which fit into and fill the cavity of the chest, excepting the small space occupied by the *heart*, the *trachea*, and the *gullet*. *(Aesophagus.)*

They are sponge-like in character, being full of small tubes and air cells.

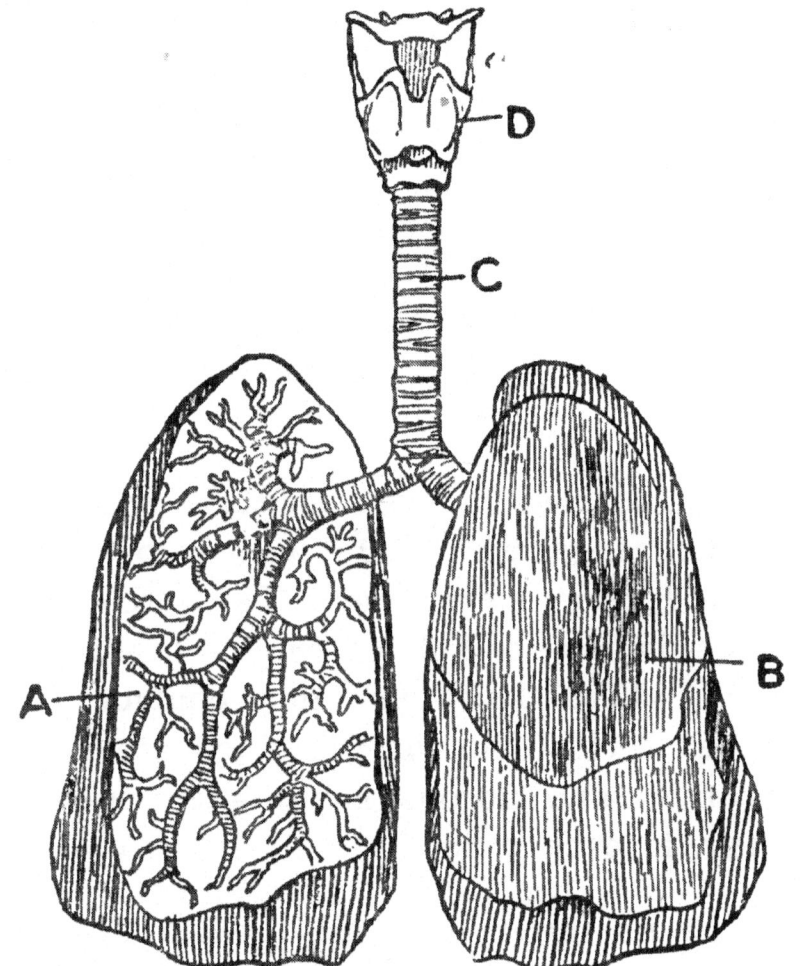

Fig. II.   The Lungs, Trachea, and Larynx.
A, Right Lung showing the Bronchial Tubes.   B, Left Lung.
C, Trachea.   D, Larynx.

Each lung is enclosed in a double-ply bag called the Pleura, (plural, Pleurae).   The inner ply of this bag adheres closely to the lungs, and the outer ply to the ribs.

The lungs are passive, and depend, for the performance of their functions, on the movements of the diaphragm and ribs. (See page 30).

THE TRACHEA.

The Trachea or Wind-pipe (Fig. II., C.) is a tube which leads from the lungs to the larynx.

It is formed by eighteen or twenty cartilaginous rings, which are united to each other by a fibrous membrane. The circle of these rings is not complete, but is broken at the back, where they come into contact with the gullet. The ends of the rings are connected by the same fibrous membrane which unites them to each other.

At its lower end, the trachea divides into two tubes or branches, called the **Bronchi**, (singular Bronchus) one of which enters each lung.

When the bronchi enter the lungs, they, in turn, divide into smaller tubes, and these, again, subdivide into still smaller ones, and so on the process goes, down to the smallest tubes which are ultimately merged in the minute cells of the lungs.

The trachea is lined with a delicate mucous membrane, which also extends upwards into the pharynx and nasal cavities, and downwards into the smallest tubes and cells of the lungs. This membrane is covered with small glands secreting *mucous*, the fluid which keeps it in a moist state.

THE LARYNX.

The Larynx (Fig. II., D.) is situated at the top of the trachea, of which it might be said to form the crown.

In shape it resembles a V-shaped box, with the sharp end pointing forward and protruding in the throat.

It is composed of several cartilages of which we must consider the following :—

The CRICOID CARTILAGE,
The THYROID CARTILAGE,
The EPIGLOTTIS, and
The ARYTENOID CARTILAGES.

The Cricoid Cartilage (Fig. III., A), which is really the topmost ring of the trachea, forms the base of the larynx.

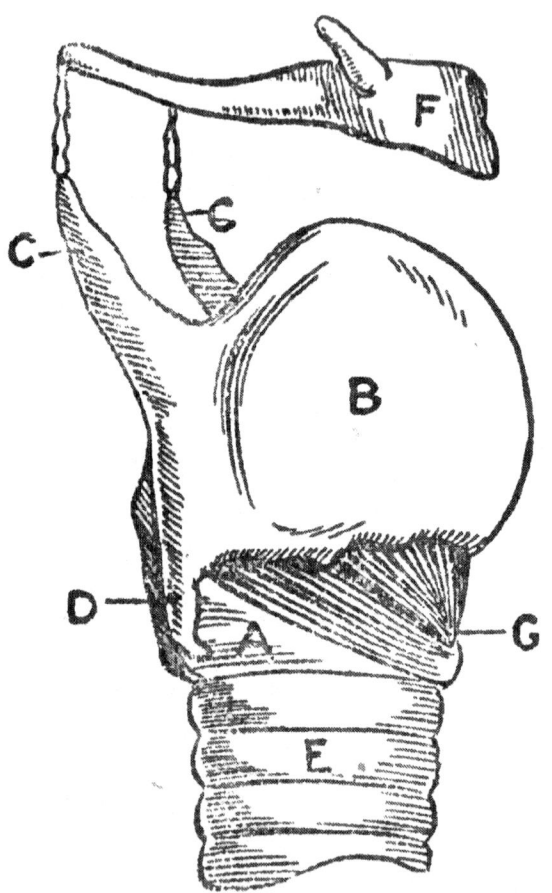

Fig III. . The Larynx—side view.
A, Cricoid Cartilage. B, Thyroid Cartilage. C, Upper Horns.
D, Lower Horn on right side. E, Upper part of Trachea.
F, Hyoid Bone. G, Crico-Thyroid Muscles.

In appearance it resembles a signet ring, with the seal or plate placed behind.

The **Thyroid Cartilage** (Fig. III., B.), is situated immediately above the cricoid cartilage, and forms the walls of the V-shaped box already referred to.

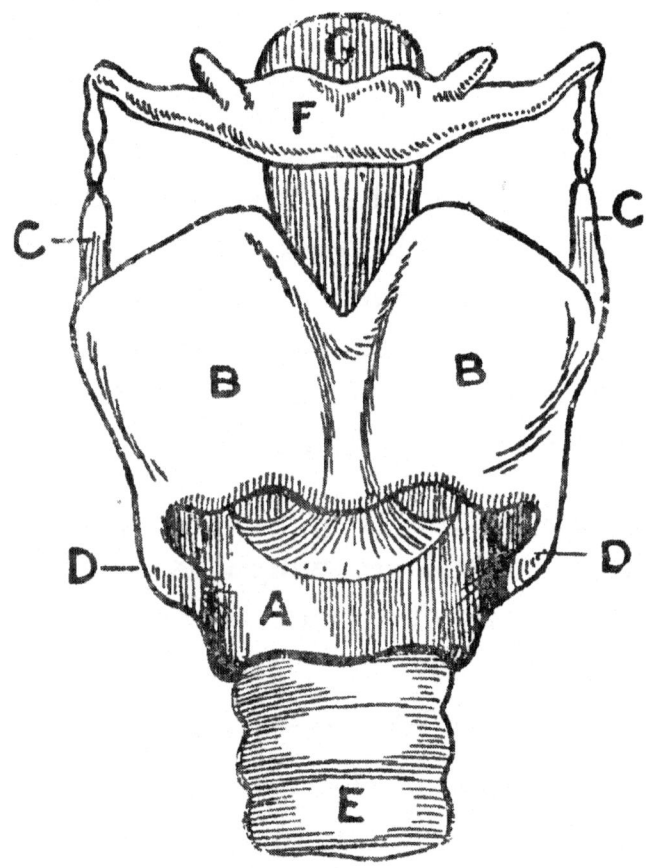

Fig. IV.   The Larynx—front view.
A, Cricoid Cartilage. B, Thyroid Cartilage. C, Upper Horns.
D, Lower Horns.   E, Upper part of Trachea.
F, Hyoid Bone. G, Epiglottis.

It is like two shields set at an angle and joined in front, (Fig. IV., B.).

There is an upper and a lower horn on either side of the Thyroid Cartilage at the back (Fig. IV., C, D.).

The upper horns are attached by cartilaginous bands to the Hyoid Bone *(Tongue Bone)*. (Fig. III. and IV., C, C.).

The lower horns (Fig. IV., D.) come down over the sides of the Cricoid Cartilage at the rear, and act as hinges, whereby *the Thyroid Cartilage may be pulled down in front.* This is a most important point, and must be borne in mind in order to understand certain processes which will be described later.

The Epiglottis (Fig. IV., G.) is a pliable leaf-shaped cartilage, which is attached at its smaller and pointed end to the inside of the Thyroid Cartilage in front. Its larger end is free, and points upwards.

The function of the epiglottis is to protect the larynx against the intrusion of any foreign substance which might enter it in the act of swallowing. This it does by coming down and closing the upper opening of the larynx, like a soft lid or cushion. Occasionally it fails to perform this duty, and then we experience the painful sensations of choking.

That the larynx has other means of protection there is no doubt, as cases have existed of people who possessed no epiglottis, and yet experienced no discomfort therefrom. In such cases the larynx is protected by the *constriction* or closing of certain parts above the vocal cords.

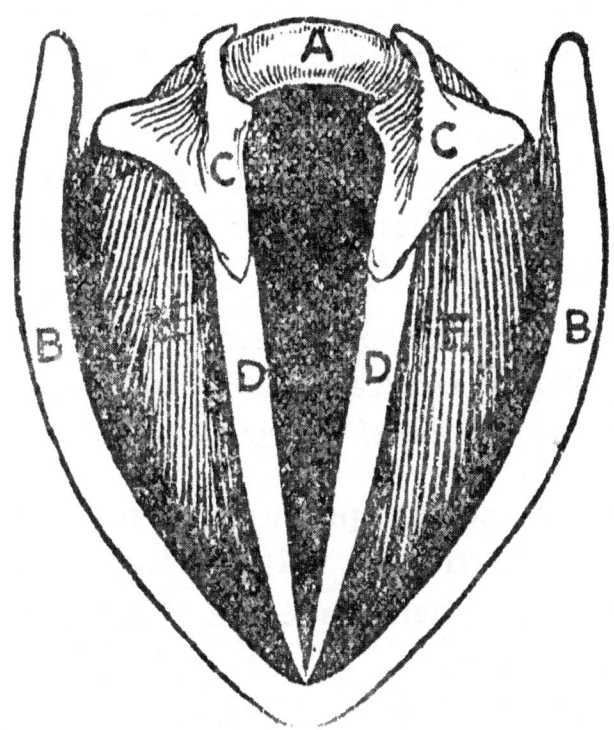

Fig. V.   Inside of the Larynx, viewed from above.
A, Back portion of Cricoid Cartilage. B, Thyroid Cartilage.
C, Arytenoid Cartilages.   D, Vocal Cords.
E, Thyro-Arytenoid Muscles.

The Arytenoid Cartilages (Fig. V., C.) are two small pyramid-shaped objects, with triangular or three-cornered bases, which are situated upon the upper rim of the cricoid cartilage at the rear.

The points of the bases reaching forward are called the **Vocal Processes**, because *the rear ends of the vocal cords are attached to them.*

The points to the right and left are called the **Muscular Processes**, because *certain muscles are attached to them.*

The arytenoid cartilages are capable of performing a peculiar *rotary or pivot-like motion upon their bases.* Thus—

If the muscular processes are *pulled forward* the cartilages *revolve inwards* in such a manner as *to bring the vocal processes close together.*

If the muscular processes are *drawn backwards*, the cartilages will *revolve in the opposite direction*, which will have the effect of *separating the vocal processes.*

We shall see, shortly, the object of these movements, also, the muscles which govern them.

The **Vocal Cords** (Fig. V., D.) are two pieces of delicate, elastic tissue which reach from the back to the front of the larynx.

They are situated inside the thyroid cartilage, and are united to it—throughout the entire length of their outer edges—by certain muscles *(Thyro-Arytenoid muscles)* which project on either side like a couple of wedges or shelves.

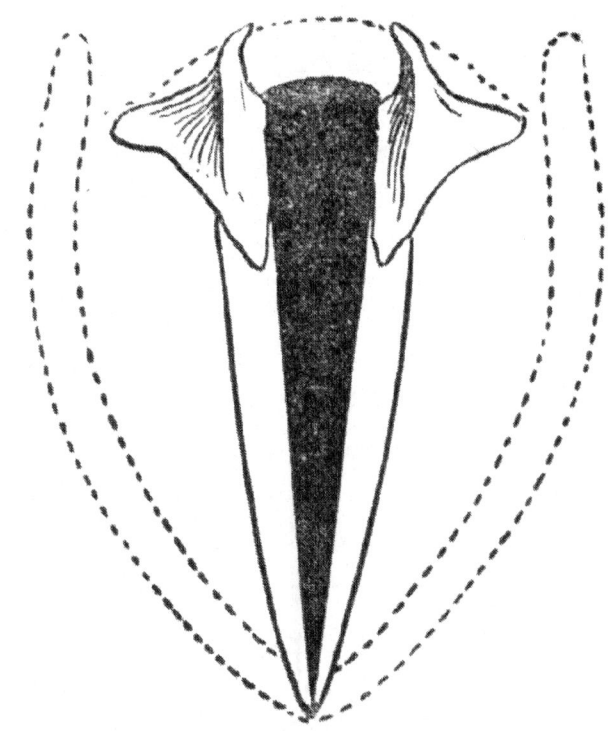

Fig. **VI.** Vocal Cords in repose.

Each of the vocal cords *is attached at its rear end to the vocal process of the arytenoid cartilage facing it.*

The *forward ends* of the cords *are attached to the thyroid cartilage in front,* where the **two** sides of the V—shaped box meet.

During respiration the vocal cords are *quite slack*, and are *separated by a considerable space* (Fig. VI.).

This space is called the Chink of the Glottis.

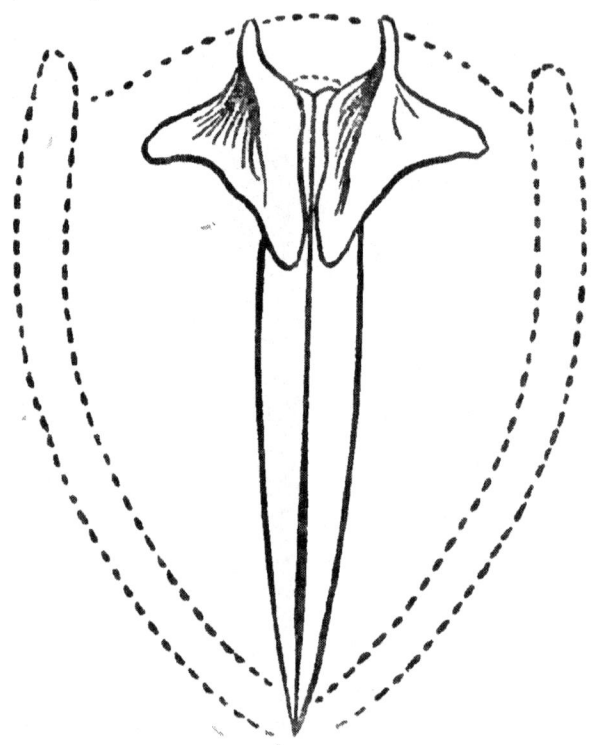

Fig. VII.   Vocal Cords in the production of sound.

In order to produce vocal sound *the cords must be stretched*, and at the same time *brought into close proximity*, so that the chink of the glottis is almost closed.   (Fig. VII.).

This condition is brought about by different sets of muscles acting upon the various cartilages of the larynx. Of these muscles we consider the following—

STRETCHING THE VOCAL CORDS. { The Crico-Thyroid Muscles, The Posterior Crico-Arytenoid Muscles.

The Crico-Thyroid Muscles (Fig. III., G.) rise in a sort of fan-shape from either side of the cricord cartilage, and are attached at their upper ends to the corresponding sides of the thyroid cartilage.

When contracted, they pull the thyro'd cartilage *down* and *forward*, and as the vocal cords are attache1 to it, *they also, of necessity, are subjected to the same downward and forward pull.*

The Posterior Crico-Arytenoid Muscles (Fig. VIII., A.) rise from the back of the cricoid cartilage, and *are attached, at their upper ends, to the rear portions of the muscular processes.*

They assist in stretching the vocal cords by *resisting the forward pull of the crico-thyroid muscles, i.e.,* they hold, and even pull back the arytenoid cartilages, to which—be it remembered—the rear ends of the vocal cords, are attached.

The vocal cords, then, are stretched by the *forward pull* of the crico - thyroid muscles, opposed by the *backward pull* of the posterior crico-arytenoid muscles.

RELAXING THE { The Thyro-Arytenoid
VOCAL CORDS {   Muscles.

The Thyro-Arytenoid Muscles (Fig. V., E.) lie along the inside walls of the thyroid cartilage, and are attached, at their posterior ends, to the arytenoid cartilages. They run behind, and parallel with, the vocal cords, of which they form the basis or foundation.

These muscles relax the vocal cords by *pulling up the thyroid cartilage* in opposition to the downward pull of the crico-thyroid muscles.

CLOSING THE ⎧ The Lateral Crico-Arytenoid
                          Muscles.
CHINK OF ⎨ The Transverse Arytenoid
THE GLOTTIS   Muscle, and
              ⎩ The Thyro-Arytenoid Muscles.

The Lateral Crico-Arytenoid Muscles (Fig. VIII., B.) arise from either side of the cricoid cartilage, and are attached above, *to the front portions of the muscular processes.*

When contracted, they pull the muscular processes forward, causing the arytenoid cartilages to revolve inwards in the manner already described; (see page 17) *thus bringing the vocal processes with the cords attached, close together,* and closing the chink of the glottis. (Fig. VII.)

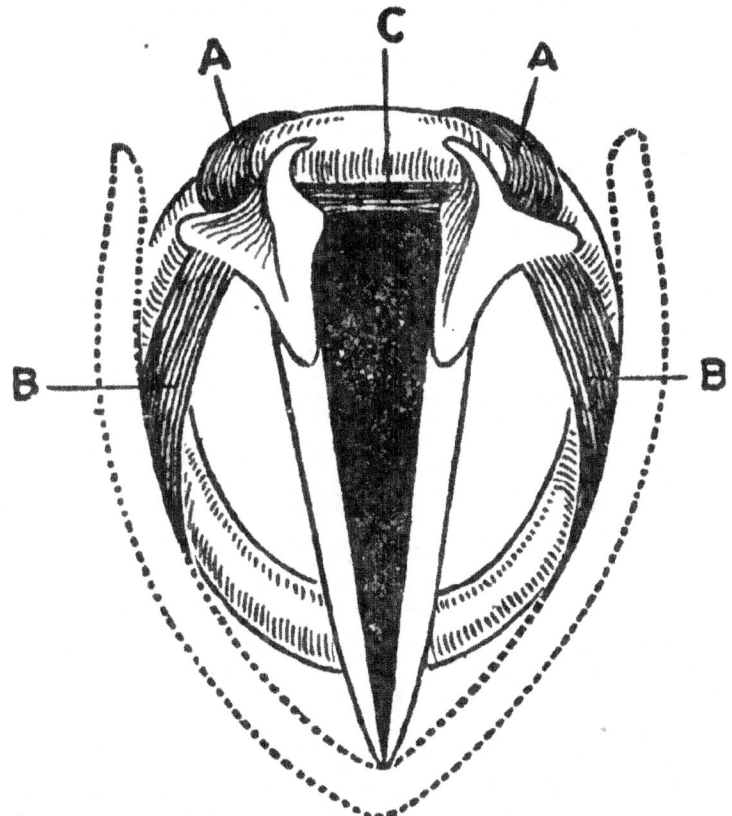

Fig. VIII.   A, Posterior Crico-Arytenoid Muscles.
B, Lateral Crico-Arytenoid Muscles.
C, Transverse Arytenoid Muscle.

The Transverse Arytenoid Muscle (Fig. VIII., C.) is a single muscle connecting the two arytenoid cartilages.

When contracted, *it draws these cartilages together*, and thus assists in closing the chink of the glottis.

The **Thyro-Arytenoid Muscles** (Fig. V., E.) in addition to relaxing the tension of the vocal cords, (see page 21) assist in closing the chink of the glottis by *compression*, *i.e.*, by pressing the vocal cords towards each other.

OPENING THE CHINK ⎰ The Posterior Crico-
OF THE GLOTTIS. ⎱   Arytenoid Muscles.

The **Posterior Crico - Arytenoid Muscles** Fig. VIII., A.) already described in connection with the stretching of the vocal cords, perform the further function of opening the chink of the glottis. This they do by acting in the opposite manner from the lateral crico-arytenoid muscles, *i.e.*, they pull the muscular processes *backwards*, causing the arytenoid cartilages to *revolve outwards*, thus *separating the vocal processes and the vocal cords*, and opening the chink of the glottis.

The action of the vocal cords in the production of sound will be dealt with under "The Voice" (page 32), and "The Registers" (page 33).

The False Cords or Ventricular Bands (Fig. IX., A.) are two loose projections, situated above, and running parallel with the *true* or vocal cords.

They are certainly not *sound producers*, though there can be no doubt that they exercise some influence upon the quality of the voice, which must come in contact with them before leaving the larynx.

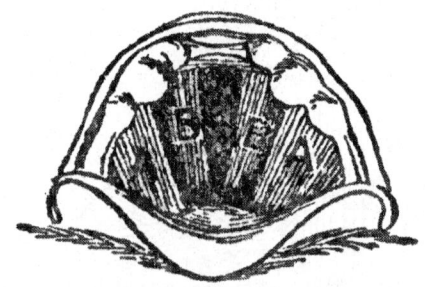

Fig. IX. A, False Cords. B, Vocal Cords.
The black shadows separating the False Cords from the Vocal Cords indicate the position of the Ventricles of Morgagni.

They assist in protecting the lower part of the larynx, and especially the vocal cords, by pressing towards each other so as to partially close the aperture between them.

The Ventricles of Morgagni (Fig. IX.) are two cavities situated on either side of the larynx, and separating the *false* from the *true cords.*

There is a little pouch or sac inside each of these cavities, filled with a mucilaginous fluid, which keeps the cords in a moistened condition.

Whatever other functions the ventricles may perform, we need only consider them in their relation to the quality of the voice; *i.e.,* as *Resonating Cavities.*

This subject will be dealt with in a later portion of the book (see page 55).

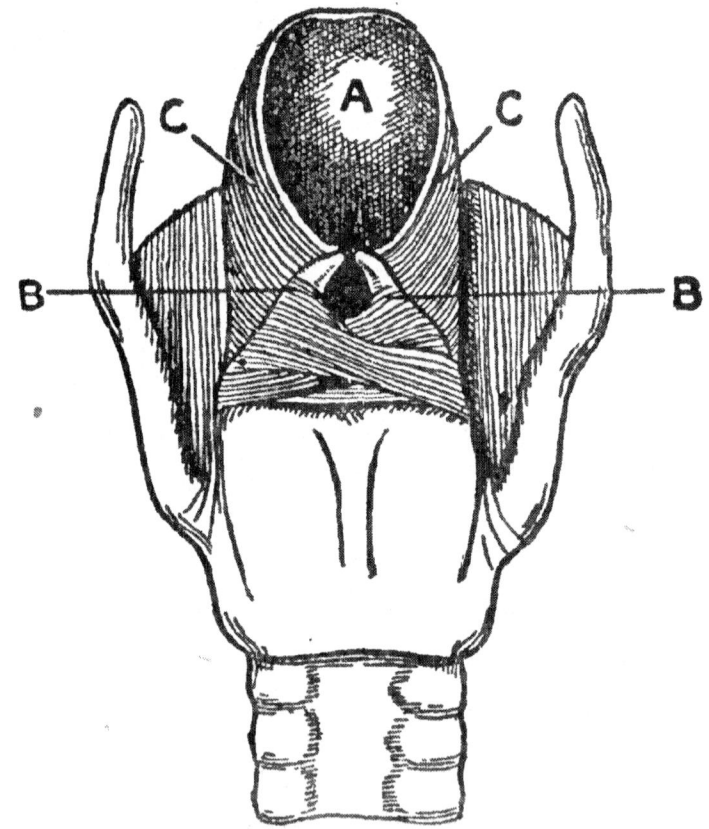

Fig. X. Back view of the Larynx showing the Vestibule. A, Epiglottis. B, Arytenoid Cartilages. C, Aryteno-Epiglottic Folds.

The Vestibule of the Larynx (Fig. X.) is a small tube leading from the larynx to the *Pharynx.*

It is formed by the epiglottis in front, the arytenoid cartilages behind, and two folds of mucous membrane *(Aryteno - Epiglottic Folds)*, one on either side, which reach from the arytenoid cartilages, forward and upward to the epiglottis.

The vestibule of the larynx is supplied with muscles by means of which it may be contracted or dilated, and it undoubtedly exercises very considerable influence upon the quality of the voice.   (page 55).

Leaving the larynx, we must now proceed to examine the various parts above.

THE PHARYNX.

The Pharynx, or upper part of the throat, is a large cavity, the major portion of which may be seen through the arch at the back of the mouth.

There are seven passages communicating with it.   These are—

1. The Gullet *(Aesophagus)*
2. The Vestibule of the Larynx
3. The Mouth *(Buccal Cavity)*

4 & 5. The passages leading to the nasal cavities *(Posterior Nares)*

6 & 7. The passages communicating between the upper part of the pharynx and the middle ear *(Eustachian Tubes)*.

The back wall of the pharynx is supplied with muscles, by means of which it may be contracted or expanded, thus altering the size and shape of the cavity.

The pharynx is the most important of all the resonating cavities, and a fuller description of its functions will be found in a later part of this book. (See page 55).

THE NASAL CAVITIES.

The Nasal Cavities are situated above the hard and soft palates, and, as already stated, communicate with the upper part of the pharynx by means of the passages which are situated behind the soft palate.

The first, and greatest function of these cavities is to heat and purify the air, before it enters the throat and lungs; but apart from this, they form a most important part of the resonator of the voice, and are, indeed, quite indispensable to its full development. (See page 55).

THE MOUTH.

The Mouth *(Buccal Cavity)* is bounded in front by the Lips, behind by the Soft Palate and Uvula, above by the Hard and Soft Palates, below by the Tongue, and at the sides by the Cheeks.

By passing the finger along the roof of the mouth, the *hard and soft palates* may be located.

The Hard Palate forms the front portion of the roof of the mouth, and is a bony structure, covered with mucous membrane.

The Soft Palate forms the back portion of the roof of the mouth, and is composed of a soft fleshy substance, which is covered by the same mucous membrane as the hard palate. In formation it resembles an arch with two ridges or pillars on either side.

These ridges are called the **Pillars of the Fauces**; the ones in front being the **Anterior**, and those behind the **Posterior Pillars**.

There are certain muscles which *raise and tighten the soft palate*, and others, which, by drawing the pillars of the fauces towards each other, *narrow the passage leading between them to the pharynx.*

The **Uvula** is the small pointed object which hangs from the centre of the soft palate. It contains a muscle, by means of which *it may be drawn upwards and backwards.*

When the soft palate is relaxed or *hanging down*, the passages leading to the nasal cavities *are open to the pharynx*, and if the voice is directed or allowed to pass through them, it will become *nasal in quality.*

As a general rule, the soft palate should be raised during singing, and this is accomplished by the muscles referred to above.

The **Tongue** is a muscular organ, which is attached to the lower jaw, and also to the hyoid bone. (See page 15.)

The **Teeth** need not be referred to, beyond stating that they play an essential part in the formation of certain consonants.

The **Mouth** is not only the *articulator*, but is also an indispensable part of the *resonator* of the voice.

BREATHING.

Respiration consists of two acts, *viz.*, Inspiration and Expiration.

During inspiration the cavity of the chest is enlarged, but there are several methods of obtaining this enlargement, of which we must consider the following:—

I. By contracting or flattening the Diaphragm. (Diaphragmatic or Abdominal Breathing.)

II. By raising, and expanding the Ribs sideways. (Lateral or Intercostal Breathing.)

III. By raising the Shoulders and Collar Bones (Clavicular Breathing).

Diaphragmatic Breathing.

In this form of breathing, the diaphragm (see page 8) contracts, and descends upon the organs contained in the abdomen, pressing them down and forward, and thus producing a bulging or distension of the abdominal wall, hence the term "Abdominal Breathing."

This method of breathing increases the capacity of the chest from *top to bottom*, and, by itself is *neither satisfactory nor sufficient.*

Lateral or Intercostal Breathing.

In this form of breathing the ribs are raised by the outer intercostal muscles. Owing to their formation, when so raised they bulge outwards, thus increasing the capacity of the chest in a *lateral direction.*

Clavicular Breathing.

In this form of breathing, the shoulders, collar bones *(Clavicles)* and upper part of the chest are raised.

Clavicular breathing is *bad*, not only for the purposes of singing, but for general health reasons, and *must be rigidly condemned.* (See page 51).

Correct Breathing.

The best method of breathing is a combination of *intercostal* and *diaphragmatic.*

If the breath be taken too deeply, thus causing excessive distension of the abdomen, *it will be impossible to obtain a free action of the ribs, and a proper expansion of the chest.*

Take breath down, until there is a slight expansion of the *upper part of the abdomen* (viz., the soft part just below the breastbone), and follow this *immediately* by pulling in the abdomen, and raising and expanding the ribs.

By means of this pulling in of the abdomen, the organs contained therein are pressed up into position, thus supporting, or as it is sometimes called, "fixing," the diaphragm. (See page 50).

Do not raise the shoulders.

Do not expand the lower part of the abdomen.

Do not hold the breath at the throat, but do so by means of the diaphragm and intercostal muscles.

THE VOICE.

The Vocal Cords, in repose, are quite slack, and the chink of the glottis is wide open.

Whenever we desire to use the voice, the cords are brought *close together*, and at the same time, are *stretched more or less, according to the pitch of the note to be sung.*

When approximated and stretched, they might be compared, in appearance, to a drum split across the centre.

The breath pressing up from below, and meeting the resistance thus formed, *forces the cords to yield a little; they then spring back and are forced up again;* and so on the process goes with lightning like rapidity, as long as the sound is sustained.

. It is in this way that the voice is produced. But this is only the beginning of the sound, which must—if it is to be of any musical value—gain power, resonance, quality, and all the attributes of good vocal tone, on its journey from the larynx to the lips.

REGISTERS.

The higher the pitch of a note, the greater will be the tension of the string or cord which produces it. As the vocal cords are only about three-quarters of an inch long in the male larynx, and considerably less in the female, it would appear that their stretching powers, and consequently their range of notes, must be very limited. Nature, however, has provided the means whereby a great compass of notes may be produced without any injurious or undue stretching.

If we consider how, on the violin, notes of different pitch may be obtained, we will find—

    1st. That strings of *equal length* but *different thickness* produce notes of widely different pitch.

2nd.   That strings of *equal length* but *different tension* produce notes of different pitch.

3rd.   That, by placing a finger on one of the strings, and thereby *reducing the length of the vibrating part,* we obtain a higher note.

Thus the pitch of the note will depend on the *length, thickness* and *tension* of the string.

Whereas the violin has four strings of different thickness and tensity, acting independently of each other, and each capable of producing its own series of tones, *the larynx has only two, which work simultaneously, producing one note at a time by their joint action.*

The mechanism of the larynx, however, is such that the vocal cords will vary not only in tension, but also in thickness and length, according to the note to be sung.

If we sing up a 'scale, beginning with the lowest notes, the cords will, at first, vibrate throughout their entire *length, breadth* and *thickness,* increasing in tension with each succeeding note, until a point is reached beyond which further stretching would be injurious.

At this point, if we allow nature to act freely, the vocal cords will be adjusted, so that only their *inner edges* can vibrate. In effect, this is similar to the change from a thick to a thin string on the violin.

It will now be possible, by means of the thinner cords, to produce a further series of tones, naturally and without strain.

In this altered condition of the cords, the stretching process will be resumed, and will continue with each higher note, till we reach, once more, the point where a further change is necessary.

In this change—by means of which the highest notes of the voice are produced—the vibrating part of the cords is *much reduced in length,* the effect being similar to that of *stopping,* or shortening the vibrating part of the violin string.

The series of tones obtained by each of the conditions described, is called a *Register.*

The first is called **Chest Register.**

The second is called **Medium Register.**

The third is called **Head Register.**

These terms are descriptive of the sensations of the singer, and refer to **Resonance**; not, as might be supposed, to the locality of production.

The subject of registers is, perhaps, the cause of more dispute than any other in voice production.

Some teachers differ as to the number of registers, while others deny their existence altogether, maintaining that the voice is, or should be, produced in one way throughout its compass.

In the perfectly produced voice there should be no apparent change. That is, there should be no *break*, and *no abrupt change of quality or timbre.*

Though this very desirable state of things may, occasionally, be found in fresh, untrained voices, and can certainly be brought about by correct training, it does not follow that the mechanism of the voice does not undergo any change, or that different registers do not exist. Rather, is it, that in the well constituted and balanced vocal organ, *the changes both of mechanism and timbre are so gradually and smoothly made,* that the voice appears to be, as in fact it is, *one perfect whole.*

As it is possible for the painter to shade his colour from blue to green, from green to yellow, and from yellow to white, so mixing and blending the shades that there is no line of demarcation ; so it is possible to mix and blend the registers of the voice, that they become one perfectly united whole.

After the foregoing, it should be unnecessary to say, that when a pupil produces the voice well, with no apparent changes of register, *the teacher must not, on any account, adopt such a method of training as will create breaks, or introduce abrupt and pronounced changes of timbre.* (See page 59).

PART II.

THE EXAMINATION.

PAPER WORK.

Candidates will receive notification of the day and hour at which they are to attend, and, should present themselves at the College a little time before the hour stated.

Each candidate is seated at a small desk, and is supplied with pen, ink, and as much paper as he may require.

As soon as one paper is completed, it should be handed to the professor in charge, who will then supply the candidate with the next.

OPTIONAL PAPER WORK.

At the examinations for the A.R.C.M. diploma, there are special papers in *(a)* Harmony, *(b)* Counterpoint, for those who desire to have a declaration on their certificates, as to a competent knowledge of either or both of these subjects.

COMPULSORY PAPER WORK.

All candidates are required to work papers on the following subjects:—

1. Rudiments of Music.

2. Figured Bass.

3. Vocal Physiology, and the Teaching of Singing.

RUDIMENTS OF MUSIC.

Candidates should study, and thoroughly master, Manhire's "First Principles of Music," which contains all the information necessary for this paper.

Papers on the Rudiments of Music and Figured Bass, set at past A.R.C.M. and L.R.A.M. examinations, may be obtained on application to the respective Secretaries, and candidates should procure a number of these and work them at home. A charge of sixpence per paper is made at the Royal Academy.

Questions are asked under the following heads:—

Time—Value of Notes, Rests, The Tie, The Dot, and the Double Dot.

Time-Signatures—Simple and Compound.

Scales—Major, Minor, (both forms) and Chromatic (two forms).

Degrees of the Scale—and Technical names for each.

Degrees of the Scale—and Triads found on each.

Key Signatures—and Related Keys.

Intervals—including Compound Intervals.

Intervals—and the Minor Keys they denote.

Intervals—and their Inversions.

The various Clefs—including Transposition from one clef to another.

Transposition of a short melody from one key to another.

Too great care cannot be exercised in working the papers.

Anything approaching *carelessness in reading the questions*, will probably lead to *mistakes in answering them*.

The following points are important, and should be carefully observed :—

Clear and legible writing.

Correct spelling of all Terms.

Answers should be Clear, Concise, and Complete.

Accuracy of Notation. This includes the Correct grouping of Notes, the position of Stems and Hooks, the order and position of Sharps or Flats in Key Signatures, the insertion and correct placing of Rests, Ties, Dots, Slurs Accidentals, etc.

Always group the notes so as to show clearly the division of the bars into beats. The same care must be taken with regard to rests.

Remember to insert Key-Signatures, unless directed otherwise.

Remember to insert Time-Signatures.

Remember to insert Clefs.

Note if Scales are to be written *ascending* or *descending*, or in *both ways*.

Note if Key-Signatures are to be used, or if sharps or flats are to be placed before the notes.

Write Scales in Semibreves, unless directed otherwise.

In writing musical examples, be careful to space the notes so that there is no crowding at any part.

Understand thoroughly the construction of all Scales—Major, Minor, and Chromatic.

Be able to define the following :—

Diatonic, Chromatic, Enharmonic, Concord, Discord, Resolution, Relative Major, Relative Minor, Tonic Major, Tonic Minor, Interval, Inversion, Triad, Common Chord, Chord of the Seventh, Dominant Seventh, Suspension, Perfect, Major, Minor, Augmented, Diminished.

Practise writing chords and short melodies in each of the clefs.

Practise transposing given phrases from one key to another.

FIGURED BASS.

This paper usually consists of five or six bars.

Soprano, Alto, and Tenor have to be added to the Figured Bass given.

Each part must be written on a separate Stave.

The C Clef is used for the Tenor Stave, but the Treble Clef is generally used for the Alto part.

The clefs to be used will be marked on the examination paper.

Be careful not to misread the figuring.

Write only the chords indicated.

Suspensions, Chords of the Seventh, and Inversions, are used.

Practise working exercises, such as are to be found in Stainer's Harmony (Novello's Primers).

VOCAL PHYSIOLOGY.

This is, undoubtedly, the most important part of the Paper examination.

As a rule there are only two or three questions, but these are of such a nature as to demand in answering, *a full exposition of the subject.*

Remember that the object of this paper is to find out how much you know of the physiology of the voice.

Make your answers *concise* but *complete.*

Be *brief*, but do not be *scanty.*

The questions are generally on the lines of the following :—

I. *What is the Motive Power used in the production of Vocal Sound?*

II. *Give a brief description of the Vocal Organs and their respective functions in Voice Production.*

III. *State the Normal Compass of each Voice, and the limits of the various Registers.*

The answers to these questions should cover, practically, the whole subject of vocal physiology.

It is not meant by this that candidates are to write an elaborate, and comprehensive treatise, but they should endeavour to *convey as much as possible*, in the limited space and time at their disposal.

All the main points should be touched on in such a manner as to show that the candidate understands his subject.

Take the questions in turn and answer them somewhat on the following lines:—

I. As to the first:

The Motive Power of Vocal Sound is the Breath.

Thereafter describe the breathing apparatus, detailing the various parts in the following order:—

Formation of the Chest or Thorax.
Inner and Outer Intercostal Muscles, and their functions.

Diaphragm, and its functions.

Lungs and Trachea.

Act of inspiration, with the movements of the Diaphragm and Ribs.

Correct method of Breathing (inspiration and expiration) for singing purposes.

II. As to the second:

Describe the vocal organs as follows:

Position and structure of the Larynx, and functions of the various Cartilages.

Vocal Cords and their attachments.

Various muscles employed in opening and closing the Chink of the Glottis, and stretching and relaxing the Vocal Cords
False Cords.

Describe the following cavities and their functions:—

The Ventricles of Morgagni,
Vestibule of the Larynx,
Pharynx,
Mouth, and
Nasal Cavities.

Describe the mouth in the formation of the main Vowel Sounds.

Classify the Consonants under their various heads, describing briefly the actions of the tongue, lips, teeth, etc., in their formation.

III. As to the third :

Draw up a table similar to the one given in Part III, (pages 61-63), showing the Compass of each Voice, and the limits of the various Registers.

NOTE.

The form of the questions may vary from year to year, but in substance they are likely to be much the same as those given above.

The candidate must not be dismayed at the amount of ground he has to cover.

Practice in writing will enable him to state his facts very concisely.

Candidates are strongly advised to devote a large amount of time to writing and re-writing papers on Vocal Physiology, in order to acquire *clearness and brevity of expression.*

PART III.

ORAL EXAMINATION.

If success is to attend the candidate in this part of his examination, it is imperative that his knowledge be practical and thorough.

Considerable as is the knowledge required to do the paper work, it will never carry one through the questioning and cross-questioning of the oral examination, *unless theoretical knowledge is backed up by practical experience.*

Candidates are expected to have had some experience in teaching, and questions are based on this assumption.

It would be difficult, if not impossible, to detail the course of the oral examination, but the following hints will be found very useful, and helpful to the candidate.

As a rule there are three examiners in the room.

They have the candidate's physiology paper before them, and may raise questions on any of the points contained therein.

The candidate is requested to treat one of the examiners as a pupil, and demonstrate upon him his method of procedure with a new pupil, who knows nothing of voice production.

We will now give a general outline of the course which should be adopted by the Candidate.

1.—Explain how you test the pupil's voice.

When you have done this, proceed to instruct the examiner upon the following points, just as you would do with a new pupil.

2.—Correct Pose.

Stand erect, but not stiffly.

Keep the shoulders well back and down.

Hold the head well up, but not thrown back.

Do not place the feet close together, but allow the one to be slightly advanced.

Look, but do not stare, at a point on a level with the eyes.

3.—Breathing Exercise. (Without voice).

> To obtain a proper expansion of the chest, advocate breathing down till a slight expansion of the upper part of the abdomen has been obtained, followed *immediately* by pulling in the abdomen and raising and expanding the ribs.

> Request the examiner to place his hands upon his sides—not low down, but *up* on the ribs—so that he may feel the movements of the chest walls.

> Emphasize the need for *mental as well as muscular control*, in order to resist the tendency of the chest walls to collapse.

Next describe a breathing exercise on the following lines:—

> Inhale *slowly*, and *evenly*, while *mentally counting four*. until a fairly full expansion of the chest is obtained; next, hold the breath quite still during a similar period of time, then slowly, and evenly, exhale during a further *count of four*.

> *The breath must be controlled and held entirely by the muscles of the chest, and the diaphragm.*

Do not tighten the throat, nor try to hold the breath there.

Express strong disapproval of clavicular breathing, stating your reasons.

If requested, be prepared to describe further exercises with, and without, voice, for the development of control over the breathing.

4.—Attack.

Explain what is meant by Attack.

Describe the "*Stroke of the Glottis*," and how you would assist pupils to obtain it.

Remember the "Stroke of the Glottis" is simply the *precise, clean,* and *instantaneous starting of the tone,* and should not be accompanied by any sound of shock or explosion in the throat.

Poise the breath momentarily, hear mentally the note to be sung, then, with the utmost quickness and lightness, attack it truly in the centre.

Do not slur up to it.

Do not allow the breath to precede the tone.

The Italian vowels A *(ah)* and E *(ai)* are the best to use at first, but ultimately all the vowels should be introduced.

5.—Sustaining single notes.
This exercise consists of one long note, sung with perfect evenness, forward placing and controlled breath.

6.—Blending of two notes.
This exercise consists of two notes, perfectly united and blended in tone colour.

7.—Blending of three or more notes.
Describe exercises similar to above extending over a third, a fourth, and a fifth.

We will now consider the *various points which may be raised*, and on which candidates *must* be prepared to answer questions.

EMISSION OF THE VOICE.

The principal qualities of a good emission are :—

Correct Attack,
True Intonation,
Steadiness of Tone, and
Beauty of Tone.

FORWARD PLACING OF THE VOICE.

While the Italian vowel A *(ah)* is the basis upon which all good vocal tone is built, it is not suited to every voice to begin with.

When difficulty is encountered in bringing the voice forward on that vowel, the following exercises should be used on different notes about the middle of the voice.

  I. *oo* or *oh*
  II. *oo < oh < ah*
  III. *ee* or *ai*
  IV. *ee < ai < ah*

In the second and fourth exercises the change from vowel to vowel must be made almost imperceptibly, and the voice must not be allowed to slip back in the mouth.

Be able to demonstrate, by singing exercises such as the above, and to explain why certain vowels are more forward than others.

QUALITY OF TONE.

Quality of tone is dependent upon the balance of ground note and overtones, *viz.*, the number of upper partials present, which of the series, and their strength relative to the ground note.

OVERTONES OR UPPER PARTIALS.

Be able to explain the difference between a *simple* and a *compound tone.*

Explain how overtones are formed. Give the series of overtones from C' up to the fifteenth harmonic.

BEAUTY OF TONE.

The following are essential to beautiful vocal tone.—

1. Correct balance of ground note and overtones.

2. Properly controlled breath.

3. Freedom from constraint, especially in the neighbourhood of the vocal organs.

4. Correct Attack.

5. Forward placing of the voice.

6. Correct use of the resonating cavities.

7. Personal perception of good tone.

THE "REACH" OR CARRYING QUALITY OF THE VOICE.

This depends upon—

1. Control over the breath. (If too much is used it will veil the tone.)

2. Forward placing.

3. Full and correct use of resonators.

4. Distinct Articulation.

AMPLITUDE OF TONE.

This depends upon the energy or force of the impact of the breath upon the vocal cords, and upon the amount and the character of the resonance imparted to the tone, after it has been generated.

RESONATING CAVITIES.

These are—

The Chest,
The Ventricles of Morgagni,
The Vestibule of the Larynx,
The Pharynx,
The Mouth, and
The Nasal Cavities.

The Chest is, as it were, the Sound Box upon which the vocal instrument stands.

The Ventricles add resonance to the tone by permitting the sound waves to expand sideways.

The Vestibule—owing to its power of contraction and dilation and to the pliable nature of the Epiglottis, which may partially or wholly close its upper opening—must exercise a very considerable effect upon the resonance.

The Pharynx may be considered the most important part of the resonator of the voice.

Not only does it gather together, and reflect the sound waves, but it plays a most important part in the production of the varying shades of *timbre* or *tone colour.*

The Mouth serves the double purpose of Resonator and Articulator.

By means of its variable cavity the different vowels are formed, while by the contact of the tongue, teeth, and lips the consonants are produced.

The Nasal Cavities are of *immense value in adding brilliance to the voice.*

TONE COLOUR.

Tone Colour and **Resonance** are inseparable.

Without Resonance there can be no colour.

The different shades of colour or quality are due to variations in the resonance employed.

Every change—however slight—in the shape or character of the resonating cavities, must, of necessity alter the relations of ground note and overtones, and, as we already know, it is upon these that quality of tone is dependent. (See page 53).

Facial expression has an important bearing upon the colour or quality of the voice.

It is impossible to produce bright, happy tone with a sombre expression of face, and equally impossible to portray sad or sombre emotions with an inane or meaningless smile.

Without varying tone colour, singing would be dull, grey and uninteresting.

The singer should be able not only to deliver his words clearly, but also to *give to each word that quality of tone which is required to make it really expressive.*

In order to do this, he must realize the force of expression contained in a word. For instance—to sing the words *love* and *hate* with the same tone colour would be, most evidently, absurd, and yet how many singers do so.

Some singers' idea of colour consists of strong contrasts in power. Probably they would endeavour to express *love* by singing piano or pianissimo, and *hate* by yelling fortissimo.

Colour has nothing to do with noise.

Sing the word *love*, trying to express, by the voice, all the sweetness and tenderness it contains.

Sing the word *hate* as though you meant it. It is not necessary to sing fortissimo in order to make this word expressive. *The utmost degree of passion may be conveyed in a whisper.*

In addition to the colour imparted to particular words, the singer must consider the song as a whole, and endeavour in it to *present to the listener a complete and beautiful picture.*

It is by the appropriate use of tone colour, that *atmosphere*—without which art is impossible—is given to the song.

REGISTERS.

A Register may be defined as,—*a series of notes, produced by the same mechanism, or condition of the vocal organs.*

Advocate the existence of three registers, *viz.,* **Chest, Medium and Head.**

All three registers are to be found in the **female voice.**

In the **male voice,** generally speaking, there is only one register, *viz.,* **Chest.** This, however, is divided into **Upper** and **Lower Chest, Upper Chest** being also called "**Mixed Voice.**"

Head Register is often used by tenors and even by baritones, in soft singing, with beautiful effect.

Be able to define "**open**" and "**closed tone.**"

Explain your method of blending registers, describing the exercises used, and the vowels found most beneficial.

Remember that while there is no fixed note on which a register must change, there *is* a note beyond which no register should be forced up.

An upper register may be carried down, but a *lower register should never be forced up.*

The equalizing of registers should be accomplished by singing exercises *from above downwards*, rather than from below upwards, for the following reasons:—

1. It is easier to change from an upper register into a lower than from a lower into an upper.

2. When changing from a lower to an upper register, there is a sudden relaxation of the vocal cords which is apt to cause a jerk or break in the voice.

3. There is less risk of straining the registers.

4. If exercises are practised from below, there is a strong tendency to force a register upwards beyond its proper limits, *thus weakening the lower notes of the next register, and greatly increasing the difficulty of a smooth junction.*

The incorrect use of the resonating cavities *is fatal to the successful blending of the registers.*

As the voice ascends in *chest register*, it should approximate more and more in quality, or resonance, to *medium register*, which, in turn, should approximate, on its upper notes, to *head*.

Allow the resonance to rise with the voice, and in this way abrupt changes of timbre will be avoided.

When descending from an upper register, introduce as much as possible of its resonance into the upper notes of the register below.

The following table shows what, in most cases, should be the limit of the registers in the various voices.

MEZZO-SOPRANO.

*CONTRALTO.

*Some so-called Contraltos

can sing up to : 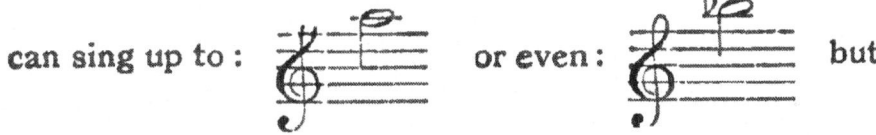 or even :   but

these are not likely to be *real* Contraltos.

TENOR. *(octave lower).*

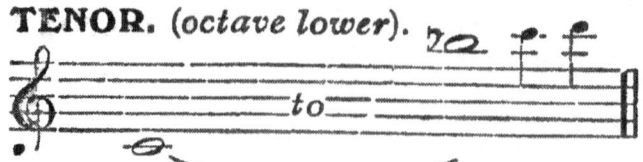

Chest.   Upper Chest (Mixed Voice).

BARITONE.

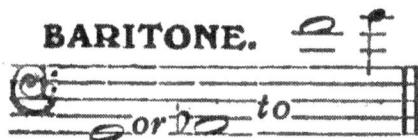

Chest.   Upper Chest (Mixed Voice.)

BASS.

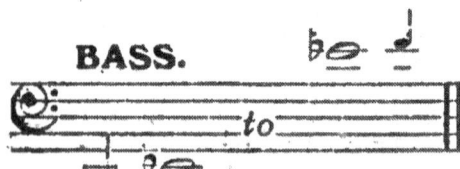

Chest.   Upper Chest (Mixed Voice).

It may be stated, as a general rule, that none of the registers should be carried above these limits. It is, however, possible, and always *very advisable, to carry an upper register downwards*, well into the compass belonging ordinarily to the register beneath. Thus sopranos should endeavour to cultivate *medium register* down to the lowest note of their compass, and *head register* well down into the domain of *medium*.

Not only is this very beneficial to the voice, but the power to use either register on these notes, greatly enhances the artistic effect of singing.

The same rule applies to all voices—male, and female.

AGE WHEN THE STUDY OF SINGING MAY COMMENCE.

Puberty in boys and girls begins about the thirteenth or fourteenth year.

During this period the larynx develops and grows, and this growth leads to an increase in the compass of the voice, and, in the case of boys, to a drop in pitch of one octave.

Owing to the changes which take place, the mucous membrane of the vocal cords becomes congested and swollen, and until all this has subsided, and the physical conditions are established, no singing should be attempted. This applies to both boys and girls, but more especially to boys.

As a rule girls may begin to study singing about the seventeenth or eighteenth year, and boys about the nineteenth or twentieth.

FIRST YEAR'S STUDY.

FIRST TERM should be devoted to the following points :—

Correct Pose,

Breathing,

Attack,

Placing, improvement, and development of the *medium register.*

When this has been satisfactorily accomplished, add one or two notes, either in *head register* or *chest register*—whichever is easier to the pupil—and blend with *medium.*

SECOND TERM. Continue to improve and develop *medium register*, and to extend the compass a *little further* either into *head* or *chest register*.

Begin the study of *Vocalizzi*, **also** advocate the use of *Solfeggi*. (Be able to name suitable Studies for each voice).

About the middle of this Term take up one or two simple *Italian Arias* and *Recitatives*. (Be able to mention several for each voice, giving keys.)

THIRD TERM. Continue the development and improvement of *medium register*, and extend the compass of the voice, both up into *head* and down into *chest*, *but on no account introduce extremely low or high notes*.

Continue the study of *Arias* and *Recitatives*, and introduce an occasional *English Song*.

(Be able to mention several for each voice, giving suitable keys. Candidates are advised not to mention songs of the modern drawing-room type.)

PREPARATION OF A SONG.

Read the words carefully through and obtain a full perception of their meaning, beauty, and atmosphere.

Commit the words to memory.

Recite them with due attention to diction, articulation, tone - colour, and dramatic expression.

Learn the melody of the Song, using *Solfeggi* to do so.

Fill in breathing, phrasing, and expression marks.

Always insert a breathing mark about one bar before the voice enters, so that the pupil may learn to *prepare the breath.*

Remember the *pose.*

Avoid a set and unnatural expression of the face. Remember that it should reflect the emotions of the song, and the singer.

Make the song interesting to the listener, both *verbally* and *musically*.

RECITATIVE.

"A species of declamatory music, **extensively** used in those portions of an opera, an oratorio, or a cantata, in which the action of the drama is too rapid, or the sentiment of the poetry too changeful, to adapt itself to the studied rhythm of a regularly constructed Aria." *Grove's Dictionary.*

Recitative may be divided into two kinds—

    I. Recitativo Secco *(unaccompanied recitative).*

    II. Recitativo Accompagnato *(accompanied recitative).*

Recitativo Secco is the form which was generally used by the old masters. It still survives, and is very largely used by modern composers.

In this class of recitative, the **singer is** quite unfettered as regards time and note values, and the whole artistic effect is dependent upon his musical and dramatic ability.

Recitativo Accompagnato, while more modern, is by no means new. It has, however, been enormously developed in more recent times, and was brought to a state of great perfection by Wagner.

Owing to the definite rhythmic form imparted by the accompaniment, the singer has not the same freedom in regard to time, as he has in *Recitativo Secco*.

In recitative, when two notes of the same pitch occur at the end of a phrase, it is customary to sing the first one as an *appoggiatura*, a tone or semitone higher, according to its position in the scale.

Recitative is strongly recommended in early studies, as it cultivates expression, tone colour, imagination, and dramatic feeling as nothing else can do.

Candidates may be asked to sing a recitative at sight, demonstrating practically their knowledge and appreciation of the above points.

STUDIES FOR FLEXIBILITY.

Be able to play from memory several exercises for flexibility, such as those contained in Garcia's "*Art of Singing*," or Randegger's "*Singing*."

Also, be able to name *Arias* and *Vocalizzi* for the same purpose.

Candidates should be able to play from memory the first two or three bars of the *Vocalizzi* named by them

When mentioning *Arias*, state keys to suit the various voices.

LENGTH OF PRACTICE.

To some extent this will depend upon the pupil, and on the condition of the voice.

Beginners should not exceed *five to ten minutes at a time,* and *twenty to thirty minutes in all, each day.*

More advanced pupils may practise *fifteen to twenty minutes at a time,* but should not exceed *one, to one-and-a-half hours in all each day.*

Never practise if the voice is in the least degree fatigued, and always stop before symptoms of fatigue begin to show.

PRONUNCIATION.

Emphasize need for the clear articulation of consonants.

Make them clear, crisp, and instantaneous.

Do not dwell upon them.

Preserve the purity of the vowels, and give them their full value in duration.

Speak your words at the lips, and not in the back of the mouth or in the throat.

Cultivate "forward placing" in speech as well as in song.

Avoid all provincialisms and vulgarisms in pronunciation.

Be able to define what a *vowel* is, and to classify the *vowels* as *simple, compound (dip- thongal), long,* and *short.*

In singing, the varying length of the vowel sounds is largely neutralized by their musical setting.

Define what a consonant is.

Explain how the various *consonants* are pro- duced, and classify them as *labials, dentals, palatals,* etc.

DICTION.

This embraces—

1. *Correct Accentuation of Words*, so as to give full meaning and force to a phrase.

2. Elocution.

3. Graceful Delivery.

4. Correctness of pronunciation.

Candidates may be asked to demonstrate their knowledge of this subject, by reading certain lines, probably the words of a recitative.

This is an important point, and it is very advisable to have some knowledge of elocution.

It is not sufficient to read the words intelligently; they must be read with due regard to tone colour and dramatic feeling.

PHRASING.

The following are the essentials of good phrasing :—

1. Sufficient knowledge of *Form* to enable one to recognise *Section*, *Phrase*, and *Sentence*.

2. Taking of breath in such places as will *best preserve both the Musical and Verbal Phrase.*

3. Sense of *Time, Rhythm,* and *Accent.*

4. Use of *Special Accent* and all the *Nuances of Musical Expression.*

EXPRESSION.

Expression demands Correct Phrasing, and in addition—

1. A musical temperament.

2. Full appreciation of the beauty of both the words and music to be sung.

3. Command over vocal technique.

EAR TESTS.

Candidates are asked to sing *intervals,* also to name *intervals* played on the pianoforte by one of the examiners.

As a rule *intervals* are within the octave, but this is not necessarily the case. *Any intervals* may be asked.

TIME AND RHYTHM TEST.

This usually consists of a few phrases played by one of the examiners, the candidate being asked to state the time of each example.

SIGHT-SINGING.

This consists, as a rule, of an *Aria,* or a portion of an *Aria,* from some unknown work. It is not a very severe test, but difficult enough to prove a stumbling-block to many candidates.

ACCOMPANYING AT SIGHT.

This consists of an accompaniment of average difficulty, and generally of fairly quick movement. It must be *played to time,* and there must be no holding back to look for notes or chords.

TRANSPOSING AT SIGHT.

This may consist of a part of the accompaniment which has just been read at sight, or it may be a different piece of about the same difficulty.

As a rule candidates are asked to transpose the piece *a tone up or down.*

MESSA DI VOCE.

Demonstrate **your** method of teaching this.

Remember it is one of the most difficult accomplishments in singing, *and should not be attempted until great command has been obtained over the breathing.*

Used on *certain notes*, the voice may pass through the various registers. Thus, a tenor might begin in *head register*, swell out and pass into *mixed voice*, then into full *open chest*, and diminish again into *head*.

THE SHAKE OR TRILL.

The following points should be emphasized:—

1. The breath must be under control.

2. The whole shake must be sung in one breath.

3. It consists of two distinct notes in rapid alternation, and must on no account be allowed to degenerate into a " wobble."

4. *The intonation must be perfect*, care being taken that the upper note does not flatten.

5. The two notes must be equal in time value.

6. When the shake occurs at the junction of two registers, *it should be sung in the upper one.*

7. The shape of the mouth should not change.

8. Practise in *medium register* only, until proficiency is acquired.

9. Practise on all the vowels.

THE CADENZA.

The Cadenzas is, more or less, of a florid character.

Usually it is introduced on a chord of the 7th or $\frac{6}{4}$, though this is by no means an invariable rule.

It may be short, and sung in one breath, or may be prolonged to considerable proportions.

As a rule it is sung on one syllable of a word, or to the exclamation—*Ah !*

The cadenza belongs distinctively to the *florid style*, and would be ridiculously out of place in the Wagnerian or more *modern style.*

It used to be the custom of singers in Italian Opera to extemporize their own Cadenzas.

VARIOUS STYLES OF SINGING.

These may be classified as follows:—

1. Canto Spianato. (Plain Style.)
2. Canto Fiorito. (Florid Style.)
3. Canto Declamato. (Declamatory Style.)

Canto Spianato is characterised by Simplicity and Nobility.

It demands *clearness of articulation, purity of diction*, and command over all gradations of *power, light and shade, legato, portamento, tempo rubato*, and, in limited degree, the use of such ornaments as the *turn* and *shake.*

Canto Fiorito abounds in all ornaments such as *trills, turns, rapid scale and arpeggio passages.*

It demands great brilliance of voice and full command of vocal technique.

Canto Declamato demands *dramatic force, intensity of passion, clearness of articulation, and diction.*

FAULTS IN VOICE PRODUCTION, THEIR CAUSE AND CURE.

As Candidates are usually asked some questions on this subject, we will refer to a few of the most common faults met with.

CLAVICULAR BREATHING.

Not only is this habit bad for voice production, but it is very injurious to the health.

The following are some of the evils which attend it :—

1. Tightening the throat in the endeavour to control the breath.

2. Throaty, or *tight* tone, consequent on this straining.

3. Breathy tone, owing to inability to restrain the flow of the breath.

4. Impossibility of obtaining an easy and natural production.

5. Tremolo.

The cure consists in practising *the correct method of breathing*, already described.

THROATY OR GUTTURAL TONE.

This is generally caused by stiffening and raising the root of the tongue in such a manner as to push back the epiglottis in the way of the sound waves.

In order to effect a cure, the following procedure should be adopted:—

1. Stand in a good light, with a hand mirror held up in front of the face.

2. Open the mouth about the width of the thumb.

3. *Do not set the jaw stiffly*, but allow it to drop easily and without constraint.

4. Notice that the tongue in repose lies *flat*.

5. Now sing *Ah* softly, on a note about the middle of the voice.

6. Exercise *will power* to keep the tongue flat, and all the surrounding parts in a loose and unconstrained condition.

7. If necessary, hold the tongue in position with the aid of a silver spoon.

8. Practise the following exercises on easy notes about the middle of the voice, gliding from vowel to vowel with as little movement of the vocal organs as possible :—

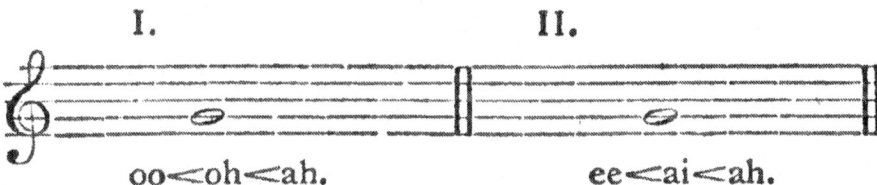

I.   II.

oo<oh<ah.   ee<ai<ah.

NASAL TONE.

Nasal tone is due to the uvula and soft palate hanging down, thus obstructing the forward placing of the voice, and causing it to pass through the nasal cavities.

To cure this—

1. Use the hand mirror and open the mouth as before, about the width of the thumb.

2. Take breath through the *nose* and notice how the *soft palate falls*.

3. Take breath through the *mouth* and notice how the *soft palate rises*.

4. Practise raising the palate by drinking in the breath through the mouth as in *yawning*.

5. Practise exercises similar to those given for the cure of *guttural tone*.

When nasal tone is due to a relaxed state of the soft palate, or to an elongated uvula, the affected parts should be painted or gargled with a strong astringent.

In aggravated cases the uvula may require to be cut by a doctor.

BREATHY TONE.

This is due to the vocal cords not being sufficiently approximated, thus allowing the breath to flow too freely and veiling the tone.

The cure consists in practising the *stroke* of the *glottis* on all the vowels in succession, but principally on the Italian vowels *i* and *e*, as these give a closer position of the cords than the others.

WEAK MIDDLE NOTES.

Some Contraltos and Mezzo-sopranos, who have excellent low and high notes, are very weak in the lower half of the *medium register.*

This indicates either, that the *chest register* is *being forced too high and produced with too heavy a resonance,* or, as is the case in breathy tone, that the *chink of the glottis is too open.*

This open condition of the chink of the glottis is often present when the voice passes from chest into medium register, and it is always accompanied by some weakening of the tone.

The following procedure should greatly improve this defect :—

1. Refrain entirely from the use of *chest register* for a time, and carry down *medium register.*

2. Using *medium register only,* practise with the *stroke of the glottis,* in precisely the same manner given for the cure of breathy tone

WHITE VOICE.

This may be described as voice devoid of *ring or resonance;* undirected and unplaced.

The cure consists in reversing that condition of things.

1. Control the breath.
2. Attack correctly.
3. Direct the voice forward in the mouth.
4. Learn to use the resonators more fully.

WRONG RESONANCE.

It sometimes happens that pupils encounter difficulty, or at least are conscious of a feeling of effort and weight, when singing the upper notes of *medium register.*

This is often due to the wrong use of the resonators.

The higher the note sung, *the higher should be the resonance used.*

If a Mezzo-soprano should attempt to sing, say, from ♭♩ *to* ♭♩ using the lower

resonance which she employs in *chest*, or even in
the *lower medium register*, she will certainly
experience this feeling of effort or oppression.

The same statement applies to male voices.

If a Baritone or Tenor should sing from about

with the same re-
sonance which he employs on the lower notes of
chest register, there will be a feeling of effort
present, the voice will become *too thick* in quality,
and will fail to obtain that brilliance which
should characterise it.

Not only is this the case, but, should too low a
resonance be used for these notes, it will create
great difficulty in obtaining good high notes.

The cure consists in a fuller use of the higher
resonating cavities, viz., the *nasal cavities*.

Help the pupil to realize the existence and use
of these, and to *avoid the employment of low
resonance on high notes*.

TREMOLO.

This is one of the worst faults to be met with in singing, and, unfortunately, it is also a common one.

It may be described as a kind of undulation or "wobbling" of the tone, amounting in fact to regular and rapid departures from, and returns to, the true note.

It is due, as a rule, to unsteadiness of the diaphragm, caused by a wrong method of breathing.

Often it is involuntary, but sometimes it is deliberately acquired under the impression that it improves, and adds expressiveness to, the voice.

The cure of this fault is difficult, and sometimes very slow.

Attention must be paid to the following points :—

1. Obtain the correct pose.

2. Avoid clavicular breathing.

3. Take breath in the correct manner already described, *fixing or supporting the diaphragm by a slight pulling in of the abdominal wall.*

4. Learn to control the breath by means of the *diaphragm* and *intercostal muscles.*

5. *Never attempt to do so at the throat.*

6. Practise sustained tones, sung softly and with perfect evenness.

7. Avoid loud singing and never force the voice.

Tremolo must not be confused with *Vibrato,* which does not entail any departure from true intonation.

A *true vibrato,* when it is the outcome of real emotion or passion, is one of the greatest charms of the artistic singer.

SLURRING.

This is a common and very objectionable fault.

When attacking a note do not slur or "scoop up" to it.

Do not slur about from note to note under the impression that you are singing *legato.*

The *Portamento*, when used artistically and with discrimination, is one of the most beautiful accomplishments of the trained singer, but it is a totally different thing from the vulgar habit of *slurring* so often heard.

SINGING OUT OF TUNE.

There are several causes for this deplorable fault, of which the principal ones are—

1. Lack of sense of pitch. (Bad ear.)

2. Forcing both the power and compass of the voice.

3. Bad production, leading to constant strain or effort.

4. Exhaustion, general, or of the vocal organs.

5. Carelessness.

6. Stiffness and lack of control over the vocal organs.

7. Forcing of the registers.

8. Inability of the mind to anticipate a note or interval before singing it.

9. Physical defect in the vocal organs.

In most cases, the last of these will be incurable. The first and eighth may, with time and care, be improved. All the others may be remedied with persevering practice *on the right lines.*

NOTE.

It must not be supposed that questions will be asked on all the points dealt with throughout this book. On the other hand, it is not to be assumed that every possible question has been dealt with.

It is the duty, and should be the desire, of all students, to know their subject *through and through*, and not simply to scrape along with the minimum of exertion and knowledge.

The object of these examinations is not the gratification of those people who desire "letters after their names," but, is to raise the standard of teaching, and to guarantee to the public, that those who hold the diplomas are competent and trustworthy teachers.

INDEX.

New Songs
For All Voices

Each 2/- net.

TITLE OF SONG.	KEYS. (And Compass of Lowest Key)	FOR WHICH VOICES MOST SUITABLE.
Aspiration	D (Bb to D), E, G, Ab...	All Voices ...
Bells of Home, The	C (B to D), D, Eb, F ...	All Voices ...
Blackbird Love	C (C to E), Eb, F ...	Mezzo-Sop., Sop.
Call of the South, The	Bb (C to F), D, Eb ..	All Voices ...
Call, The	G (D to D), Ab, Bb, Db	All Voices ...
Caprice	Bb (C to D), C, D, Eb	All Voices ...
Carolling at Toon, The	C (C to E), D, E ...	All Voices ...
Dance Away	Bb (Bb to F), C, D ...	Mezzo-Sop., Sop.
Fifinella	Ab (Bb to Eb), Bb C, D	Bass-Bar., Tenor..
Garden of Forgetting, The	G (C# to D), Ab, Bb, C	All Voices ...
In a Monastery Garden	Eb (Bb to Eb), F, G ...	All Voices ...
Joy Bird, The	Db (Bb to Db), Eb, F, G	All Voices ...
Little Dutch Garden, The	C (C to F), Eb	All Voices ...
Little Lamp at the Window, The ...	F (C to D), G, Ab ...	All Voices ...
Love Divine	C (A to E), Db, Eb, F...	All Voices ...
Man's Song, A	C (B to E), Db, F ...	Bass-Bar., Tenor..
Memories at Eventide...	C (C to D), D, Eb, F.	All Voices ...
O Day Divine	C (B to E), Db, Eb, F...	All Voices ...
Over Jordan	F (C to D), G, Bb ...	Bass-Bar., Tenor..
Passers-By	F, (C to Db), G, A ...	All Voices ...
Pearl of the West	Db (Ab to Db), Eb, F...	Cont., Mezzo-Sop.
Pearls	C mi. (Bb to Ab), D mi.	Mezzo-Sop., Sop.
Sing in the Dawn	C (C to G), D, Eb ...	All Voices ...
Song of Comfort, A (Sung by Dame Clara Butt)	C (B to C), Eb, G ...	Cont., Mezzo-Sop.
Song-Time and Dawning	Ab (Bb to Eb), Bb, C, Db	All Voices ...
Street of Quiet Windows, The ...	C (C to F), D, Eb, F ...	All Voices ...
Sword of Old Japan, The	Fmi. (C to Db), Gmi, Bbmi.	Bass-Bar., Tenor..
There is always a Moment	G (D to D), Ab, Bb ...	...
Wonderful World of your Heart ...	D (Db to Eb), Eb, F ...	All Voices ...
Yonder (Sung by Dame Clara Butt)...	C mi. (G to E), C# mi , Eb mi., F mi. ...	All Voices ...

J. H. LARWAY

HERBERT OLIVER
SONG CYCLES.

				Price.	
BELLE OF THE BALL, THE					
Operette Cycle			...	6	0
CRIES OF LONDON, THE					
Suite for Sop. Solo, Chorus and Orch. ...			...	2	0
Separate Parts (O.N.) S.A.T.B.			...	0	4
Tonic Sol-fa Edition			...	1	0
Arr. for Female Voices S.S.C. each part ...			...	0	4
Arr. for Male Voices, T.T.B.B. each part ...			...	0	4
(Orchestral and Vocal Parts may be hired.)					
EIGHT BALLADETTES.					
Low. High			...	3	6
FIVE LITTLE MASCOTS.					
Low. Med. High			...	3	6
LYRICS OF LONDON.					
Low. Med. High			...	3	6
MY LADY'S CHARMS.					
Low. Med. High, ...			...	3	6
OUR PANTOMIME.					
Quartette Cycle			...	5	0
PASSING SHOW, THE					
Quartette Cycle			...	5	0
SONGS OF AVARAIR.					
Low. High			...	3	6
SONGS OF THE DEVON MOORS.					
Low. Med. High				3	6
SONGS OF THE KING'S COURT.					
Bass. Baritone			...	3	6
SONGS OF MERRIE ENGLAND.					
Low. Med. High			...	3	6
SONGS OF THE NORTHERN HILLS.					
Low. High			...	3	6
SONGS OF OLD LONDON.					
Low. Med. High			...	4	0
SONGS OF THE ORIENT.					
Low. Med. High			...	3	6
SONGS FROM A SICILIAN GARDEN.					
Low. High			...	3	6
THREE PERSIAN SONGS.					
Low. Med. High			...	3	0

J. H. LARWAY, 14, Wells St., Oxford St., London, W.1.

LBW. No. 98.

CPSIA information can be obtained at www.ICGtesting.com
Printed in the USA
BVOW08s1015131014

370572BV00021B/660/P